#BrandYourself

Professional Branding through Business Etiquette

Table of Contents

Introduction 1

Chapter 1: Technical Ability vs. Promotability 7

Chapter 2: Appearance and Presentation 11

Chapter 3: Effective Communication 23

Chapter 4: Dining 29

Chapter 5: Classy Finishing Touches 31

Chapter 6: Reputation Management Strategy: Impressions and Perceptions 39

Chapter 7: Impressions 43

Chapter 8: Perception 47

Chapter 9: Steps to a Reputation Management Strategy 51

Chapter 10: Authentic Connections 59

Chapter 11: Authentic Brand 65

Chapter 12: The Networking Formula 71

Chapter 13: Online Networking 77

Chapter 14: Networking Action Plan: 81

Chapter 15: Differentiation (Unique Value Proposition) 87

Conclusion 93

About the Author 95

MEMORABLE QUOTE

"Your Brand is what other people say about you when you are not in the room."
-Jeff Bezos

D YOURSELF

Introduction

Have you mastered (or even heard of) the unwritten rules of success? In today's competitive job market, you can't get ahead without being privy to these unwritten rules. You won't find these rules in a college course or text book, but you are expected to know them the day you decide to look for a new job, new customer, or client. You will be judged, hired, and promoted based on how well you apply these rules to your corporate career.

This book will expose the tools, tips, and guidelines you will need to #BrandYourself professionally. It will help you get the job, keep the job, and climb the corporate ladder of success quickly and efficiently. Whether you are a young professional, corporate climber, or entrepreneur, this book will show you how to attract new business and job opportunities.

With the branding and business etiquette skills you develop from this book, you will be ready to turn existing clients into returning clients who will readily refer you to everyone in their network. A chron.com article stated the "…mastery of business etiquette can help even small businesses hold their own against their larger and more high-profile competitors."

As a stubborn "learn the hard way" type of learner, I was forced to become a student of all the business etiquette courses and books I could get my hands on. I have tested and modernized the principles featured in this book in order to #Brand myself professionally, shape my career, and propel to levels of corporate and client management. This would have never happened without these principles.

Young professionals, corporate climbers, and entrepreneurs have all benefitted from applying the rules of branding and business etiquette to enhance their career and expedite its upward trajectory. As evidenced by the number of major corporations hiring etiquette speakers, corporate America sees the value in preserving its brand, reputation, and client relationships and provides this training to its employees. Imagine as a young professional, the leg up you will have if you knew and applied these tips from day one!

Will this guidance work? I wish I was equipped with this knowledge when I graduated college. I graduated when I was 20 years old and went straight to law school where I was expected to network with corporate professionals, recruiters, and senior management. I was required to navigate my way through interviews, information sessions, networking events, and dinners with classmates, colleagues, professors, and potential employers.

Little did I know, my brand and lack of business etiquette skills were on full display and I was being judged not only on my networking capabilities, which needed work, but also on my ability to order the correct wine to accompany my meal. It wasn't until I was pulled aside by a professor when I realized that I was unknowingly jeopardizing opportunities by committing a few faux pas. Knowing the proper rules of business etiquette and professional branding could have prevented many embarrassing moments.

The best thing about a guidebook like this is that the principles and tips can be applied immediately. You can begin to #Brand Yourself professionally and measure effectiveness from your first interview to your first client and beyond.

If you use the tools, work through the assessments, and implement these tips then you will be equipped with strategies and tactics that will give you a competitive advantage in today's job market. You will get the job, impress the clients, and climb the corporate success ladder quicker than your colleague who may lack the posh principles you will become privy to in this book.

Don't stall your progress or delay your opportunities by being a person who does not know what you don't know! Be the corporate climber who others look to as the model of success — the person nominated as 'Most Likely to Succeed.'

The business etiquette and professional branding tips you are about to read and apply have been proven to make an impactful impression that lasts long after you leave the room. They will keep you as the front runner in a company and ensure you always stay on the client's mind. All you have to do to gain this advantage is keep reading.

#BrandYourself is composed of five sections for each letter of your BRAND:
- **B**usiness Etiquette,
- **R**eputation Management,
- **A**uthenticity,
- **N**etworking, and
- **D**ifferentiation.

Each section will present insightful chapters, self-assessments, posh principles, and actionable steps to take. Take control of your career path now, gain a strategic competitive advantage, and enjoy the corporate climb.

SECTION 1

Business Etiquette

Chapter 1: Technical Ability vs. Promotability

In college, you had the opportunity to gain the technical skills and abilities to carry out tasks and perform a job or career successfully. These technical abilities are deemed "hard skills" because the successful performance of these skills can be measured and quantified. Hard skills are classified as knowledge and abilities — technical proficiencies that can be taught to others and developed over time. All college graduates enter the job market with a set of hard skills that can be applied to their industry of choice. These hard skills may get graduates an interview, but they don't necessarily make you valuable, hirable, or promotable.

Although a graduate is deemed the 'best and the brightest' when they master these skills, it is not enough to make you unique and valuable. In today's competitive job market, everyone has the hard skills and they are competing with one another for the same jobs. CareerBuilder's 2017 national study of 2,380 hiring managers and Human Resources professionals in the private sector across industries and company sizes revealed that although they are eager to hire recent graduates, they are concerned that new college grads lack interpersonal or people skills (50%) or problem-solving skills (45%). These statistics support the notion that technical ability can get you an interview but soft skills will help you get and keep the job.

"Soft skills" focus on behavior, communication, appearance and presentation, emotional intelligence, conflict management, and problem solving, to name a few. It is a collection of interpersonal qualities that can positively enhance business relationships, establish trust, develop credibility, foster respect, and impress with class, sophistication, and manners. The most successful leaders and those who excel in their careers do so because of their highly developed soft skills.

Personal branding through business etiquette will equip you, the college graduate, with the tools needed to develop interpersonal attributes in the business setting. Having a personal brand will allow you to stand out in the sea of resumes and interviews from similarly situated individuals. As an avid user of business etiquette, you will transcend career changes and remain steadfast as you progress from entry-level to c-suite executive.

This section will focus on business etiquette in the following areas:

- **Appearance and Presentation:** Unfortunately, the saying "don't judge a book by its cover" is not applied in the business setting. Attire, grooming, and body language all contribute to first impressions. We will discuss the evolution of these practices as you transition from college to corporate America.

- **Effective Communication:** Written and spoken word, when communicated clearly and concisely, can set you apart as a leader and a trusted collaborator. Conversation is an art form and listening is a key component. This section will walk you through the art of conversation.

- **Dining:** Business is often solidified over lunch or dinner. Seamless navigation of business lunches, networking events, and other social encounters when dealing with colleagues and clients will ensure mishaps are avoided and lasting impressions are made.

~ Classy Finishing Touches: Small thoughtful actions can leave lasting impressions and to future business opportunities. People tend to do business with and recommend business to people they like and remember. These classy finishing touches will ensure you are at the top of the list for future business opportunities.

Chapter 2: Appearance and Presentation

Similar to a company's logo, your first representation of your brand is your appearance. You control the image you project to the world. Good or bad, that image will always be associated with your brand. Appearance alone won't brand you professionally, but it is a complement to highly developed interpersonal attributes affecting 5behavior and impacting both social and professional relationships.

APPEARANCE SELF-AWARENESS SURVEY

1. Do you invest in quality instead of quantity?

    ☐ All of the Time   ☐ Most of the Time
    ☐ Some of the Time   ☐ None of the Time

2. Do you take the time to iron and steam clothes before wearing?

    ☐ All of the Time   ☐ Most of the Time
    ☐ Some of the Time   ☐ None of the Time

3. Are you confident in your body type and what fits the best to boost your image?

    ☐ All of the Time   ☐ Most of the Time
    ☐ Some of the Time   ☐ None of the Time

4. Is your hair always neat? Nails always clean and never chipped? Cologne or perfume not overwhelming?

    ☐ All of the Time   ☐ Most of the Time
    ☐ Some of the Time   ☐ None of the Time

5. Do you stand up straight, maintain eye contact, and keep a pleasant resting face at all times?

    ☐ All of the Time   ☐ Most of the Time
    ☐ Some of the Time   ☐ None of the Time

6. Do you dress for the occasion and know when to be fashionable and flashy versus when to be classic and sophisticated?

    ☐ All of the Time   ☐ Most of the Time
    ☐ Some of the Time   ☐ None of the Time

If your answer is yes to all these questions, there is no need to read on. You're an expert at projecting the best image at all times and are ready to take on corporate colleagues from any industry. If you could honestly brush up on some tips to better position your 'book cover', read on to ensure the message you are sending through your appearance is 'judged' appropriately.

Attire:

Posh Principle:

"You can walk the walk and talk the talk, but if you don't look the part, you may not get cast for it."

-Posh Principle #1

Your appearance speaks louder than your words.

Example: Jennifer was slated to graduate at the top of her class. During her last semester, she was actively being interviewed by conservative corporate firms. Although she prepared and walked away feeling confident in her communication, she never seemed to get a job offer. After a series of denial letters, she followed up with one interviewer who told her that although she seemed to be quite competent, she didn't make the interviewer confident that she would project the image of the firm in front of clients and colleagues. Jennifer, who took pride in her trendy fashion sense didn't understand until she read the final comment which stated she should consider wearing less jewelry and lower heals as the clanking of both proved distracting and it was hard to take her seriously.

You don't have to change who you are, your sense of style, or trendy fashion sense when you enter corporate America. All you need to do is become keenly aware of your audience, the occasion, and the message you want to communicate. All three should contribute to your wardrobe choices each day.

ATTIRE

3 THINGS TO CONSIDER

1

AUDIENCE
Who will you be
seeing?

2

OCCASSION
Where will you
be going?

3

MESSAGING
What message
do you want to
convey?

Transitioning from college to corporate America requires a shift in how you think about your wardrobe. What you wear and how you wear it can communicate more about you than the words you speak. You send a loud and clear message to the world every time you get dressed. Jacqueline Whitmore, author of *Business Class: Etiquette Essentials for Success at Work* believes that people unconsciously form judgments about your background, socio-economic status, level of education, and personality traits based on what you are wearing.

Appearance can enhance your brand and influence first impressions. It can even help you get your foot in the door. With websites, such as LinkedIn, a potential employer or contact can not only review your credentials, but also your appearance. Putting together a polished package will increase the chances of a positive hiring decision.

Quality over Quantity: Quality does not necessarily translate into brands and labels. Quality means being aware of the fabric, fit, and color. Fabric, such as wool, silk, and cotton tend to be the most sustainable and the easiest to care for. Fit is specific to your body type and having an understanding of your current figure will help you choose complementary clothes. Bright colors tend to communicate 'loud' while darker colors convey confidence and authority. Neutrals are always a good investment as they can be accentuated with color. Build your wardrobe slowly and buy clothing that can be mixed and matched. Good quality clothes and shoes don't wear out as fast and make for good long-term investment pieces.

Accessories:

Posh Principle:

"An accessory can be your trademark, but remember, they are silent additions. They should not overpower or distract."

-Posh Principle #2

Save the bangles and bracelets for outings with friends. Accessories are integral and can communicate your fashion sense, if done wisely. Look for classic, timeless, sophisticated pieces that will complement your style rather than pieces that will distract from it.

- **Shoes:** Shoes are always the first thing people notice about a person because they are always on display. Quality prevails here and you should invest a bit more on shoes that go with multiple wardrobe staples. The shoes should always be in good condition, fit comfortably, and complement your clothing. Women should keep the heels at a medium height. Men should keep the shoes polished.

- **Jewelry:** In conservative companies, jewelry should be classic and elegant. In moderation, jewelry can complete an outfit. In trendier professions, you will have more latitude, but be sure to choose jewelry that truly complements the outfit. People always tend to notice watches and you should wear the best quality pieces you can afford. For women, brooches and silk scarves can be conversation starters. For men, ties and belts should always be utilized.

- Bags: Time to retire the backpacks. Briefcases and handbags should be inventoried to ensure your pieces are appropriate for the season and in good shape. A briefcase and handbag can communicate style and confidence or can communicate the opposite if they are not kept in good condition.

Business is never casual

Posh Principle:

"Even in a business casual setting, whether you are the presenter or the interviewee, it is best to err on the side of being one step above the dress code. It will communicate that you take your role seriously."

-Posh Principle #3

Many companies allow business casual, but remember, business is never casual. Before you are hired, you should dress for the job you want to obtain. What you wear for leisure should not be worn to a networking event or interview. There is, however, a fine line between over and under dressing. By not dressing for the occasion, you can convey a lack of respect for others in attendance. Look at what other people are wearing. If you are unsure of the dress code, ask. It is better to be informed and prepared than to show up and make the wrong impression.

Additionally, all business casual is not created equal. Rules vary for both men and women. Again, remember the three rules of choosing the most appropriate attire — audience, occasion, and message. They apply to both business formal and business casual attire decisions.

Though the business suit is the piece of clothing that commands the most authority, there is a hierarchy to business attire. The table below shows you the hierarchy for women and men, from formal to casual.

WOMEN

AND

MEN

DRESSING GUIDELINES

Business Formal

- Business Suit (skirt or pant suit)
- Dress (no jacket)
- Jacket and Skirts (Mix and Match)

- Business Suit
- Long sleeved shirt (button down or V-neck) with pants

Business Casual

- Skirt/Pants w/blouse (no jacket)

- Khakis and Polo

Sexy is not Sophisticated:

Barbara Patcher, author of *New Rules at Work: 79 Etiquette Tips, Tools and Techniques to Get Ahead and Stay Ahead*, tells us to ask ourselves, "What do you want to be remembered for?" If your outfit is not in line with the message you want to send, change your outfit. This applies to any corporate related events even if the event is in an off-site location. Never wear anything too tight, see-through, mini, or that reveals too much cleavage. Women can be feminine without exposing body parts un-necessarily. This also applies to men, keep your shirt buttoned up. An exposed chest does not communicate competence or sophistication.

Grooming:

Grooming requires paying attention to details because if you fail to, others will notice and may even be offended. People think of grooming as hair, nails, and breath, but it is so much more.

Posh Principle:

"Conduct all of your grooming activities in private. This includes reapplying makeup and lipstick, cleaning your teeth, clipping your nails, and applying lotional to a body part other than your hands."

-Posh Principle #4

Scents: Scents, such as cologne and perfume should be subtle. Overpowering scents can overwhelm a room and, in some cases, ignite allergic reactions. Apply it sparingly as you don't want to be remembered as the guy that smelled like… you get the point.

Hair: Hair should be clean and styled. Women should wear styles that are flattering to their features. Men should keep their hair neat and trimmed, regardless of the chosen style. This includes facial and nose hair. Showing up with greasy hair or hair shedding from dandruff can be distracting and will communicate lack of care. Alternatively, arriving with wet hair is unprofessional. Playing with your hair during a meeting or interview can be distracting so, don't do this.

Nails: Both men and women should keep their nails clean and trimmed. Women, if you wear polish, keep it neatly manicured. Once it starts chipping, it is time to re-do it. You want to reassure your clients and company that you pay attention and care about the details.

Breath: Mints. Need I say more.

Makeup: Makeup should enhance your features, but should not be heavy. Use makeup to give a finished look; don't use it as a mask.

Body Language:

Body language includes your posture, facial expression, eye contact, and gestures. It can communicate assertiveness and confidence or insecurity and standoffishness. People read into your body language and tend to draw conclusions about your feelings toward them. Are you approachable and inviting or do you want to be left alone? All of this is communicated, often unknowingly, through your body language.

Posture: Sit and stand tall. Shoulders pulled back, head up and chin leveled. If standing, evenly disperse weight on both feet. This communicates assertiveness and confidence.

Facial Expression: The acronym RBF was developed by pop culture icons to explain the expression on one's face when it is in resting position. Be sure that when your face is at rest it maintains a pleasant expression. An expression that is too serious can communicate that you are upset or offended by what is going on. Be aware of what your face is communicating and, if necessary, practice a pleasant resting facial expression.

Eye Contact: Maintain eye contact to communicate that you are actively listening. Failure to maintain eye contact communicates a lack of interest and/or nervousness, neither of which you want to communicate to a potential employer.

Gestures: Gestures can work for or against you. Used effectively, gestures can add emphasis to your communication. It is important, however, to be aware of nervous gestures which can be distracting or offensive and can turn your audience off.

Positive Gestures:
- Talking with your hands within your sphere of influence.
- Smiling.

Negative Gestures:
- Folding arms in front of your chest.
- Pointing with one finger.
- Tapping nails on a table.
- Looking at your watch every few seconds.

Chapter 3: Effective Communication

To communicate well, both your written and spoken communication must be made effectively. Keep in mind that communication includes what you say to and receive from others. Active listening, fear diction, and formal grammar all contribute to effective communication. This section will explore both spoken and written communication.

Spoken Communication

Posh Principle:

"Know when to be heard, be silent, and be succinct. Use it wisely."

-Posh Principle #5

Listening Effectively: Conversation is an art form. When you are getting to know others or networking to grow your network and brand, it is important to establish valuable relationships with potential employers, clients, and customers. Establishing a valuable genuine relationship is the key. People tend to do business, make recommendations, and hire people they know, trust, and like.

When meeting new people, one way to make a good impression is to listen more than you speak and remember details. Listening more than you speak is a classy, unselfish act which communicates that you are truly interested in the other person. Remembering details about a person communicates that you want to keep them in your network on a long-term basis. Following up with them can solidify a relationship and generate future business opportunities.

Interruptions: A gracious listener does not interrupt others while they are speaking. This is a habit many people have and it will require thoughtful practice to break it. Effective listening requires you to listen to understand rather than listen to respond.

When you are listening to respond you are drafting your response in your head while the other person is still talking. You are subconsciously drawing conclusions about what you think the other person is going to say and you formulate your response before they have competed it. This results in interrupted conversations which ultimately communicates that you believe what you have to say is far more important that what the person is saying. Not only is this rude, but is ineffective in establishing relationships and branding yourself as a person who has the ability to serve the needs of others by listening and understanding their needs before drawing conclusions and providing input.

Be Heard: Have you even been a part of a group conversation or meeting where your voice is not heard? Maybe you spoke up but were ignored. Did you ever wonder why? Well, maybe it is because no one can hear you. Volume, tone, and diction all contribute to whether or not you can be heard effectively. To be heard loud and clear try these tips:

Speech: Volume, Diction, and Tone

- Volume: Avoid loud shrill sounds while speaking. Lowering your pitch will result in a pleasing sound which can be clearly heard. Posture can affect the sound of your voice. Sitting or standing up straight with your chin leveled will allow the voice to easily travel and prevents constriction.

- Diction: It is often said, "It is not what you say but how you say it." This notion is true, especially when you are fighting to be heard. Careless relaxed speech is not well-groomed speech. In communicating a polished brand, you want to communicate in a polished way. This will require you to:

  - Avoid slang.
  - Pay attention so you don't slip over consonants like L or R.
  - Relax your lip and jaw when speaking.
  - Avoid speaking through clenched teeth.

- Tone: Monotony and speed both affect the tone of your voice. Have you ever sat through a class or speech where the speaker is monotonous? What about a speech that was delivered too fast? Both should be avoided at all costs in order to be heard. A slow confident pace will not strain your voice. Adding enthusiasm to your words or a smile as you speak can help avoid monotony.

Be Silent

Guard your tongue. There is more power in thoughtful silence than we give credit for. Thoughtful silence can communicate pensive thoughtfulness. It communicates that you heard what the other person has stated and are giving it thought before responding. Be careful with this technique as the poor use of it can inadvertently communicate that you are ignoring the speaker.

Be Succinct

Don't say in a paragraph what you can say in a sentence. Long drawn out statements can exhaust and bore the listener. This goes for written and spoken word. Many people respond in long drawn out narratives because they are thinking out loud. Pause and think before responding to avoid this faux pas. You don't want to give the impression that you are over talking because you like the sound of your own voice.

Written Communication

Email: Email is the primary form of business communication. When seeking to brand yourself professionally to either obtain a new job, develop business contacts, or acquire new clients, it is important to #BrandYourself by following these posh principles:

- Use a Professional Email Address: Create an email address just for business networking. Use your name or company name and avoid catch phrases at all costs. You want to ensure the recipient knows who you are just from your email address. Inappropriate names may get you classified as spam and your email may end up in the trash.

- Customized Email Signature: Every email should contain consistent, standard language after the signature. The language should include your phone number, address, and social media links (if applicable).

- Use Formalities: Use a formal greeting before diving into the content of the message. Close all emails with a formality before the signature.

- Spellcheck and Proofread: Spellcheck each message, but do not rely solely on the built-in spell check in your email. Spellcheck only corrects the words it assumes you intended to write. Read your email out loud before sending it to check for tone and context.

Chapter 4: Dining

Posh Principle:

"When conducting business while dining, don't lose sight of the purpose of the meeting. Treat it like a business meeting, not a social dining experience."

-Posh Principle #6

Some of the most successful business deals are closed at restaurants or other off-site work events where food and drinks are served. Employers, clients, and customers put great importance on dining etiquette as it relates to social skills and professional branding. Companies rely on clients and customers and they may require employees to interact with clients and customers. Before trusting employees to meet with clients outside of an office setting, such as a restaurant, many companies tend to host dinner or lunch interviews, receptions, and networking events to screen potential candidates based on their social and dining skills.

Dining Etiquette Tips:

- You are there for business, not for food: When dining while conducting business, remember that you will be judged on your dining etiquette and professionalism. A dinner or lunch interview is a test. The relaxed setting is not an invitation to relax and let your guard down. A networking reception is not the place to get tipsy and a dinner interview is not about indulging on someone else's dime. You are being tested on your ability to navigate the rules of dining, engage on a personal and professional level, and maintain competence and business sophistication despite the setting.

- Be prepared: Prepare like you would for an interview or business meeting. Check the address of the location, driving directions, and travel time to ensure you arrive on time. Research the restaurant to learn the type of food they serve and communicate any dietary restrictions, if necessary. Dress for the meeting, not for the setting.

- Mind your manners: You will be judged on your behavior, so the basics apply. Don't over indulge or order the most expensive item on the menu. Navigate the table setting like a pro and practice beforehand to avoid blunders. Don't groom yourself at the table (i.e., lipstick application or teeth picking), silence your cell phone, make small talk in between business conversation to get to know each other, and finally, do not overindulge in alcohol.

Chapter 5: Classy Finishing Touches

"Small acts, such as sending a handwritten thank you note or discretely paying a bill, can leave a big impression that most will never forget."

-Posh Principle #7

To truly make yourself memorable and leave an impression, you will need to exercise some classy finishing touches and small acts of service. This leaves such a powerful impression in the minds of the receiver because people crave meaningful experiences, but fail to have them regularly. Small acts of service can make a big impact. When used correctly, it leaves a memorable impression on them and they will look at you as valuable, recommendable, and hirable.

Thank You Notes: After someone interviews you, recommends you, spends time investing in your career, or just does something nice for you and your career goals, it is always important to follow up with a handwritten thank you note. Get some nice stationary and write 2-3 sentences expressing your gratitude. Mail the note so the receiver can get it soon after the experience. In many instances, a handwritten note is preferable over an email as a makes a notable impression. Many hiring managers and professional contacts make decisions based on receiving handwritten thank you notes. Additionally, many people tend to keep these notes and will remember you long after the meeting, increasing your chances of obtaining a future recommendation or opportunity.

Paying the bill: If you invite a contact out for a business meeting, informational interview, or for any reason to increase your business network, you should pay the bill. It is a classy move to pay the bill by giving the restaurant the card before your guests arrive so the bill never gets to the table. This allows you to avoid any awkwardness when the bill arrives and smoothly transition to the end of the meal. You can also excuse yourself as the meal is coming to a close and take care of the bill away from the table after reviewing it. In both instances, it is best to handle it away from the guests. This will send a message you value them and you are investing in the relationship. They, in turn, may invest in you resulting in business opportunities.

Stand and Shake: When meeting someone, introducing others, or being introduced, it is always important to stand and shake their hand. You will be surprised how many people forget to stand up when meeting a new person. If one or more people are seated, it is important for all parties to stand while being introduced or making an introduction. When shaking hands, be firm. Do not offer a limp handshake nor should you shake too hard — it is not a strength competition. Instead, accept the other hand and firmly interlock while shaking with confidence.

Business Cards: Everyone should keep business cards with current information, including name, title, phone number, and social media profiles pertaining to the business at hand. Keep your cards in good condition without frayed or bent edges. A business card case will prevent mishaps and will communicate a polished image when you take a card out of the case. Do not network just to get your business cards in everyone's hands. That will communicate a shallow, vain intent rather than aid in developing a true genuine relationship. Doing this might also get your card thrown away.

When you receive a card, make sure you store it in a separate case from the one where your personal cards are stored. You do not want to give away someone else's card by mistake. It is also a good idea to jot down 2-3 things about the person giving you the card so you can remember details about them when you follow up. Carry a nice pen so when you take it out to make notes, it will contribute to your polished image.

Follow-Up: Many people meet others and fail to follow up. Don't be like those people. If you commit to following up after the initial meeting, do this within 24-48 hours. If you commit to delivering a service or connecting others, that should be done shortly after the initial meeting. This will solidify your value because following up allows a relationship to grow and develop, it allows you to become valuable as you contribute to the life of the person, and it allows others to think of you when future business opportunities arise.

Eye Contact: Similar to the 'Stand and Shake', eye contact is critical to communicating confidence and success in business. Maintaining eye contact with those you are speaking with will demonstrate that you are paying attention and truly interested in the conversation. Looking around the room or over the speaker's shoulder will communicate the exact opposite and can ruin the business relationship as the other person may take offense. Maintain eye contact with everyone you engage in conversation with to deepen the connection with those you come in contact with.

Conversation, Charm & Congeniality: There is an art to conversation. So much so that whole books have been written about it. Like professional branding, you won't find many college courses on the art of conversations, but the notion rings true that success or failure happens one conversation at a time. *How to Win Friends and Influence People* author Dale Carnegie explains the concept of "bridge building dialogue" which requires you to begin all conversations with what matters to the other person.

It starts by listening and assessing what the other person's needs are. Ask questions that require more than a yes or no response. Continue to follow up with questions until you have fully assessed the things that are important to their person then you can contribute to the conversation in a meaningful way. This is a charming and congenial way to assessing the interests of others and provide value by appealing to those interests. This will encourage true engagement and meaningful long-term dialogue in your business relationships.

Your reputation is a set of beliefs generally held about you based on a set of characteristics and behaviors. You have a reputation, whether you create it yourself or you allow others to create a reputation, good or bad. As you develop from an individual into a brand, you want to intentionally manage your reputation. You want to be in a position to manage what others think of when they think of you.

It starts with identifying how you want others to perceive you and then working towards being that person every day. This is not about being fake or putting on a show. It is about growing into the person you want to become and intentionally emulating those behaviors every single day.

The reputation of your brand should reflect your personality and your goals. It includes the business etiquette advice from the previous section along with the authenticity advice in the next. This section will dive into how you can become aware of the reputation you want to maintain personally and professionally and how you can shape what you project to the world to make good impressions and ensure that others perceive you how you intend   to   be.

SECTION 2

#BRAND YOURSELF

Reputation Management

Chapter 6: Reputation Management Strategy: Impressions and Perceptions

Just like every company and brand, as you develop your own professional brand, you will need a solid reputation management strategy. A reputation management strategy is the process of actively monitoring the reputation of an individual, brand, or company. It includes:

- Tracking your own actions,
- Controlling the message that you send to the world, and
- Managing the response of others.

It is your responsibility to maintain a certain impression. As you build your brand, you should be impressing upon others that you can be trusted and you are competent and capable of achieving the goals you are trying to accomplish. This is the impression portion of or your reputation management strategy. Your appearance, behavior, and how you treat others can contribute to the impression you make and how you are perceived.

Impressions work in tandem with perception because it influences what others think of you, which ultimately becomes their perception of you. It is often stated that perception is reality, which holds true in business and personal affairs. The way others perceive you becomes their truth about who they think you are and what they think you can accomplish. You are whatever others perceive you to be, whether it is true or not.

Both impression and perception management are crucial components of your reputation management strategy.

Posh Principle:

"Impressions + Perception = Your Reputation. Manage it wisely."

-Posh Principle #8

Know what you are projecting to the world:

The first step in your reputation management strategy is to know who and what you want to project to the world. Know what you want your target market to think of when they think of you. Think of the characteristics that would benefit your chosen line of work.

Use this exercise to answer these questions for your own personal and professional brand.

WHAT YOU ARE PROJECTING?

1. Choose a person, real or fictional, celebrity or otherwise that you admire. Write out the characteristics of the person.

2. Categorize those characteristics into Professionalism, Appearance, Feel/Presence, and Speech.

PROFESSIONALISM   APPEARANCE

FEEL/PRESENCE   SPEECH

3. Think about your goals. Do these characteristics align with your professional goals?

☐ All of the Time
☐ Most of the Time
☐ Some of the Time
☐ None of the Time

Daily Exercise:
Each day, take one characteristic from each box and practice it. The goal is to practice these characteristics until they become inherently who you are and what your brand is associated with.

Chapter 7: Impressions

We all consciously and subconsciously judge others based on their appearance, professionalism (or lack thereof), speech, attitude, and demeanor. Judgments are usually made during the first interaction with a person and are based on the first impression of them. The second step in your reputation management strategy is make a good first impression.

As you develop your professional brand, it is important to treat every interaction as meaningful. This will ensure that you will lead with your best self. Follow the advice from the Business Etiquette section, but mainly ensure you utilize these important tips:

~ Stand and shake: Stand when you are introduced and have a firm handshake.

~ Make and maintain eye contact: Maintain eye contact when speaking to others to demonstrate you are truly engage and to communicate that they are the focus of your attention at the moment.

~ Show a genuine interest in others, remember details, and make a connection: Make it your goal to truly connect with everyone you meet. Do not make it your priority to meet everyone in the room. Those relationships can quickly become shallow and you can be seen as an opportunist. A few true relationships can get you further as people can truly get to know you, connect with you, and recommend you for future opportunities. Remember, people like to do business with people who they know and like.

~ Be aware of your body language: This is the silent form of communication and can speak louder than words. Remember to have an approachable demeanor, straight posture, a pleasant resting face, and smile.

~ Follow up and send thank you notes: There is an art to following up. If you made a true connection with a potential business contact, be sure to schedule a time to talk before leaving the conversation. It is not enough to leave the conversation with a business card only. Schedule a follow up call or meeting then follow through. If someone does something for you, either through an informational interview, a job interview, or a lunch meeting, send a written thank you card. It is a nice small touch that can go a long way in making a large impression.

~ Practice the art of conversation, charm, and congeniality: Be pleasant, ask follow up questions, talk about the other person (not yourself), laugh at yourself not others, and always smile.

Be Prepared and Be on Time

There are two critical actions that could immediately lead to a positive or negative first impression and these are easy to implement: Preparedness and Timeliness. Being prepared and being on time are two things that can make or break a professional interaction. Being prepared eliminates stress and anxiety usually associated with the lack thereof. It allows you to think clearly and communicate effectively because you have anticipated much of how the interaction will go. Being on time communicates that you respect and value the time others have offered to spend with you. These are two actions that require very little effort and can give you an advantage over the competition who may be lacking in one or both of these areas.

Impressions aren't only made in person but also online. Many possible employers, clients, and customers will google you to check your profile on all the social media platforms. Everyday billions of names are searched on Google and many job recruiters are required to look up potential employees online during the hiring process. It is not rare for people to find something in an online search that made them decide not to do business with someone. The impression you make online can and will transcend to your professional brand. It is important to inventory what your online brand is communicating and align it with the reputation you are developing for to #BrandYourself.

Chapter 8: Perception

How are you perceived? Have you ever asked a friend what they truly thought about you? Use this exercise to measure the current state of perceptions about you.

Personal Relationships: What do your friends say about you? Ask 2-3 friends what they think about you then ask them what other people say about you. Do not take their responses personally. Use their responses to analyze how you are currently perceived by your friends and how you want to be perceived by your friends. You can then identify ways to close the gap.

Professional Relationships: What do your colleagues, customers, and clients say about you? Ask a lateral colleague and someone you manage or mentor how they perceive you. Ask for an objective assessment on things you can improve on. If you have ever been in the position to receive a performance review, you can gain some insight into how your boss or manager perceives you and areas that can be improved on. If you have never received a performance review, ask a professor for an honest objective assessment. Use their responses to analyze how you are currently perceived in a professional setting and identify opportunities for improvement.

Online Reputation: What does your online presence say about you? Have you ever googled yourself? Is your LinkedIn up to date? Does your Twitter, Facebook, and other social platforms align in messaging and with the image you want to present to the world? Google yourself and take note of what the top ten results say about you. If there are any negative portrayals, you should take note and find ways to change your online presence to align with the image you want to portray.

Perception cannot be controlled, but it can be managed. It starts with understanding how other people currently perceive you and how your behavior, image, and treatment of others have influenced that perception. You can fix your behavior, polish your image, and treat others better to make better impressions on others and change the perception other have of you.

People vs. Product: Reputation Management Strategy Compared

Just like how companies have reputation management strategies, you will need to also. Companies are incentivized to create reputation management strategies because they understand the importance of public perception and the impact to the bottom line. Before making purchasing decisions, consumers tend to search for reviews or look for recommendations. The reputation of a company's product or service is readily available online and companies understand that people do business with companies based on recommendations and a good reputation leads to good recommendations.

Similarly, you are incentivized to create a reputation management strategy because your public perception will contribute to whether a company, client, or colleague will do business with you, hire you, or recommend you. Your perception is influenced by both your in-person network and your online presence. People in your network are connected and you want to be aware of what they are saying about you.

An online reputation management public relations company known as repfixes.com established 9 noteworthy platforms that are crucial to a reputation management plan:

9 Platforms of a Reputation Management Plan

1. DO YOUR JOB WELL
2. KNOW YOUR FACTS
3. USE SALESMANSHIP
4. KEEP PROMISES
5. BE SINCERE
6. BE INTERESTED
7. GAIN RECOGNITION
8. BE HUMAN
9. WIN CONFIDENCE

#BRANDYOURSELF
Adapted from repfixes.com

Chapter 9: Steps to a Reputation Management Strategy

3 Steps to a Reputation Management Strategy

1 — EVALUATE

2 — PROJECT

3 — MONITOR

#BRANDYOURSELF

Evaluate: Evaluate your current reputation. Assess how your image, behavior, and the way you treat others contribute to the impression you are making. Analyze how it is affecting the perception people have of you. Consider how this affects both online and in person reputations and target ways to improve your reputation to be in line with the professional brand you are creating.

Use the exercises above to assess the current state of your reputation by speaking to friends and colleagues and conduct online research to find out what google says about you. Once you have a good assessment, you can develop a plan to close the gap between what your current reputation is and what you want your brand reputation to be.

Use the chart below to complete this evaluation.

REPUTATION
EVALUATION

1. Ask 2 friends to describe you with 3 adjectives.
   Document what they say:

   FRIEND 1   FRIEND 2

2. Ask 2 colleagues, professors, or classmates who only know
   you professionally to describe you with 3 adjectives.

   CONTACT 1   CONTACT 2

3. Are the above descriptors close to the goal from the last
   activity where you documented the person you want to be?

   ☐ Very close: With minimal effort, I will be able to get
      my brand to my goal.

   ☐ Somewhat close.

   ☐ Not close: I need a major overhaul.

REPUTATION
EVALUATION

4. Assess your online reputation.

Now , Google yourself and document what you find.

Assess your online reputation by reading the top 10 results, assessing whether the results accurately reflect who you are, and determine whether the information is positive or negative.

Summarize your findings below:

Top 10 Google Results	Positive	Negative
	☐	☐
	☐	☐
	☐	☐
	☐	☐
	☐	☐
	☐	☐
	☐	☐
	☐	☐
	☐	☐
	☐	☐

REPUTATION EVALUATION

5. Assess whether your online platforms align with your goals.

Assess your online platforms and Social Media content to determine whether it aligns with your brand goals.

Summarize your findings and whether the results are positive or negative below:

Social Media Platform	Results	Positive	Negative
LinkedIn		☐	☐
Facebook		☐	☐
Instagram		☐	☐
Pinterest		☐	☐
Twitter		☐	☐
Blogs		☐	☐
YouTube		☐	☐

Now that you have assessed your current in-person and online reputation, create a plan to improve your brand and align your message across all online platforms and in all in-person interaction (personal and professional).

Project: How do you want to be perceived? If you completed the first exercise in this section, you are equipped with a clear vision of who you want to be and what you want to present to the world. Nick Brown, the author of *How to Brand your Professional Profile* explains reputation management in terms of a "positioning strategy". A positioning strategy will allow you to assess how others currently perceive you so you can better manage your brand to influence how you are viewed when you walk in a room or when your name is mentioned.

- In Person: When you are networking and connecting with others in your profession, make sure to project the professional brand image you want to be associated with. As you aim to form true genuine connections and expand your network, you want to ensure that you will be remembered for your brand. Project the image and behavior that reflect the characteristics you deemed important to your brand at the beginning of this chapter. Be consistent and leave others with enough information to recognize you as a valuable asset.

- If you have been in a position where you made a bad first impression or the perception held is less than stellar, you will want to work on changing that perception. You will need to spend more time with any person who holds negative perceptions of you. As you spend time and project your professional brand, you may be able to change your reputation with that person.

- Online: Similar to your in-person interactions, your online presence should consistently reflect what you and your brand stands for. In his book Nick Brown stresses the importance of your online presence consistently reflecting your brand. He emphasizes the importance of online and in-person consistency so when you are Googled, they find a consistent brand message.

If you Google yourself and find negative content in the top ten search results then it is your job to produce and project new positive content that outranks the negative. You can even reach out to Google to ask that the content be removed. You also want to ensure that your social media content reflects positive images of your brand. Refrain from negativity and start producing content related to your industry. Remember, your image online can outlive you so, going forward it is up to you to project the image you want associated with your brand.

Monitor: Now that you have evaluated your current state, developed a plan to close the gap, and are projecting your brand in all settings and on all platforms, it is up to you to monitor that your positive professional brand is not changing or being tarnished. Monitor your activity and if you make a mistake, spend more time with people to improve your reputation.

It is especially important to monitor your activity and the activity of others online. As you expand your online network, be sure to monitor what other people post about you. Some platforms allow you to approve or disapprove content posted about you from showing on your own online pages. Set up alerts to receive anything you may be tagged in and before approving the content, ensure it aligns with your professional brand messaging. Future business opportunities are dependent on the monitoring of your brand.

Implementing a successful reputation management strategy is a long-term process that reaps great rewards. It requires a disciplined application of business etiquette tips, impression and perception rules, and authenticity. Your professional brand is based on how other people perceive you and your reputation reflects that perception. Although discipline, practice, and perseverance are required, a professional brand with a great reputation will make you valuable in the competitive job market and will lead to business opportunities.

Chapter 10: Authentic Connections

Authenticity has become the buzz word in branding. The word, which has so much meaning but no depth has become overused to the point of becoming trite. Many people use the word to define themselves and their brand without supporting it by their actions. It isn't enough to claim you are authentic, you must be authentic, live it every day, and allow it to transcend into your professional brand.

What is Authenticity?

Authenticity is a conscious decision to be a real and honest expression of your true self in all that you do. Authenticity builds trust as it allows others to see who you really are. It makes you relatable and gives other permission to show their true selves. It won't leave room for someone to question your motive because you are showing a true display of yourself without putting on a show. As you grow and evolve into a professional brand by applying the tips in this book, it is important to allow others to see your true authentic personality in your behavior, image, and brand.

Being authentic means staying true to who you are, identifying the core skills which comes naturally, and applying them to your career goals while building your professional brand. It must be the core of your which means that your brand should be built around   who   you   are.

SECTION 3

#BRAND

Authenticity

YOURSELF

"Authenticity is the daily practice of letting go of who we think we are supposed to be and embracing who we are."

       – Brene Brown

Authentic Connections

Both the Business Etiquette and Reputation sections of the book focus on forming genuine connections with people you meet. Being genuine is another word for authentic. A genuine connection requires you to be thoughtful, honest, and consistent in each professional interaction you encounter. Consistency is key because it is an opportunity to align your brand message with who you truly are.

Each interaction is an opportunity to demonstrate your authenticity by being engaging, stimulating, personality-packed, and uniquely interesting. This will allow you to connect with others on a human level and gives others permission to take their mask off and let their true selves be seen. Genuine connection requires you to thoughtfully listen, be sincere in your communications, and be compassionate and empathetic in your actions.

Genuine connections allow you to build credibility and integrity. People will connect with you before they connect with what you are selling. Regardless of whether you are marketing your skill set to obtain a job or if you are marking your products and services to obtain clients and customers, people will connect with you first. If a genuine connection is formed, it will be easier to obtain business opportunities because people like to do business with people they like and connect with.

Integrity is built if you live your brand and practice what you preach. You can demonstrate your skills and exert your value by practicing and living the very things that you are selling. If your brand is built with your authentic self at the core, it will be complemented by your efforts to develop your business etiquette skills and manage your reputation. These three skills will establish a trustworthy, credible, professional brand.

Chapter 11: Authentic Brand

Don't try to copy someone else's brand identity. Make the core of your brand true to you and apply the necessary skills of business etiquette and reputation management to grow your brand's network and differentiate yourself. It starts with knowing your strengths and weaknesses, in addition to your inherent and learned skills to best position your professional brand identity as authentic.

Being authentic requires showing the world the real you. As you #BrandYourself think of how you can show the world who you are and what you can do while standing out from the crowd.

BRAND AUTHENTICITY ACTIVITY

Being authentic requires showing the world the real you. As you #BrandYourself think of how you can show the world who you are and what you can do while standing out from the crowd.

1. What are your top 3 values? This can include your faith, family, career, passions, etc. List them below.

TOP 3 VALUES

2. Vision Board

   Think about your future as it pertains to your ideal career and your ideal life. What does it look like? Who is in it? What is your position or title? What industry do you work in? Use the answers to these questions to create a vision board.

   This can be created digitally in a platform like Pinterest or physically by gathering magazines and newspapers and cutting out the images that speak most to the responses to these questions. The creation of a physical representation of your future will help you see yourself in that role and speak to it when defining your authentic self.

BRAND AUTHENTICITY ACTIVITY

3. Develop your expertise. This should align with your career goals.

What is your career goal?

What is your skill set?

How do the above responses align? What do you need to do to get to your goals? What steps will you have to take before you become an expert in your industry?

BRAND AUTHENTICITY ACTIVITY

4. What is your personal branding statement? Answer the following questions:

Intertwine details of your life with your career goals. Carefully choose the details you want to share and try to relate them to your goals. What have you accomplished? Have you overcome challenges to get to where you are? How have your experiences contributed to where you want to go?

Use your responses to the above questions and the below example to develop your personal brand statement (2-3 sentences).

Personal brand statement example:

I speak to college students, young professionals, and small business entrepreneurs about branding themselves professionally and using business etiquette to set themselves apart. Corporate America is competitive and professionals need more than a degree and experience to gain business opportunities.

Your personal brand statement:

SECTION 4

#BRAND YOURSELF

Networking

Chapter 12: The Networking Formula

Networking is universally agreed upon as one of the most effective ways to grow your career or business. It allows you to build a network of professional contacts while marketing yourself as a professional brand. It provides opportunities to exchange information with people in your field. As you learn about your colleagues and their career paths, providing information and feedback can be beneficial to others.

For some, networking in a room full of strangers can be intimidating. However, it is a crucial step toward growing your professional brand and should not be avoided. Cocktail parties, corporate social gatherings, happy hours, and other events have become commonplace to connect with current, former, and potential colleagues.

Joining professional associations within your industry or volunteering within your community are great ways to start connecting with like-minded professionals. Recruiters may have events for candidates seeking opportunities with their companies and you must go. Not only will you connect with others, but you will have the opportunity to showcase your refined business etiquette, establish your reputation, and build your professional brand. Networking is a powerful strategy in brand positioning and reputation building.

If you hate the idea of mingling in a room full of strangers, you are in good company. Most people would rather stay in for an evening of 'Netflix and Chill,' but that won't help you or your brand to become visible. Visibility is the key to networking because you need other people to know who you are and what you have to offer. As your professional network grows and you become more visible, your business opportunities will also grow. Colleagues will think of you when they come across industry opportunities. They may refer clients and friends to you. They may even refer you to companies who are looking for the valuable talent you have to offer.

Networking, however, is a long-term strategy. Your professional contacts and relationships won't occur overnight. Networking to build professional contacts is like preparing for an emergency—you must build it before you need it. If you are networking with the immediate goal of obtaining a job, it is already too late.

A common faux pas is the pushy networker who attends events with the intent of passing out as many business cards as possible hoping to get a job offer. Not only is this ineffective, but it also turns most people off. It becomes evident that the person is seeking to obtain as much as possible from the people he/she just met without investing any effort to truly connect with others. Networking is the strategy you should implement in order to develop the genuine connections discussed in the previous chapters. Genuine connects require patience and time.

The Networking Formula
The Networking Formula requires preparation, organization, connection, and follow-up.

4 Part Networking Formula

1 — PREPARATION

2 — ORGANIZATION

3 — CONNECTION

4 — FOLLOW-UP

#BRANDYOURSELF

Preparation:

- When attending a networking event, know the purpose of the event, a few things about the host, and who is expected to attend. If you don't know who will be in attendance, research the industry the attendees are from and prepare discussion points around those topics. The more talking points you have the easier it will be to connect.

- Prepare an elevator speech to highlight who you are and what you have to offer. The speech should be no longer than 30-45 seconds and should be unique to you and your brand. A word to the wise, do not lead with your elevator speech. Respond with it when asked about yourself. The most effective strategy in networking is to listen more than you speak. Enter conversation, ask questions, and listen, but be prepared with the elevator speech so you can thoroughly respond when asked about yourself.

  - Example Elevator Speech:
    "I work with millennial college graduates to help them obtain a competitive advantage in the job marketplace to get their dream job and move up the corporate ladder quickly and efficiently. I was

recently working with recent college graduates who were great academic students but who were competing for a job against other top tier graduates. I helped them brand themselves professionally through the use of business etiquette and networking strategies. As a result, they quickly expanded their professional network, formed genuine connections, left good impressions on hiring managers, and obtained competitive job packages in their respective fields. I am Sabrina Michelle and I am a professional branding and business etiquette coach."

~ 3 Components of an Elevator Speech:

3 Components of a Good Elevator Speech

1 **Who are you and what do you do?**
This should include your name, the college you graduated from, the degree you obtained, or the experience that validates your expertise.

2 **What are you seeking?**
This should include your career goals. Whether you are looking for a job or business opportunity, new clients, or referrals and recommendations, include this when articulating what you are seeking.

3 **What value do you provide?**
This should include your skills and describe how you can benefit them or their organization. Think about what you can offer to appeal to their needs. Include any solutions or services you can provide to meet their goals.

#BRANDYOURSELF

~ Remember to follow the rules of business etiquette. Offer a firm handshake when you are introduced, let your attire match the occasion and the audience, remember names, and maintain approachable body language.

Organization:

~ Keep professional business cards on you at all times. They should be carried in a card case and be kept separate from the cards you receive from others.

~ When receiving cards, be sure to write a few details about the person on the back of the card. This will assist you in retaining memorable details which can be useful when following up.

~ Get to know people before offering your business card. Gauge whether a connection has been made and (if appropriate) offer your card when the conversation is ending.

Connection:

~ Do not ask about job opportunities or request favors from people you just met at a networking event. The intent of networking is to connect, exchange information with people in your field, and allow others to get to know you and your brand.

~ Create mutually beneficial relationships. Although you should not ask for favors during the initial meeting, you should connect with the right people who may be able to help you in the future and who you may be able to help in the future.

~ Be intellectually curious about others and their thoughts and ideas on the topic of discussion. Be genuine in your curiosity and it will foster a connection and develop potential long-term relationships.

Follow-Up:

Posh Principle:

"Follow-up should be in the form of a handwritten note. If time is of the essence, send an email, but never forget to follow up."

-Posh Principle #10

~ Gracefully end conversations with those you are connected with by making plans for future connection or follow-up. Planning for future follow up makes the long-term networking strategy effective because it will solidify the intent of wanting the relationship to go beyond the initial meeting. Schedule a meeting, commit to sending an email with something of value based on your discussion, and at the very least, connect on LinkedIn.

~ Follow-up within 72 hours when they are still fresh in your mind, and hopefully you're in theirs.

~ Set a follow-up goal for each contact you make. Know where you would like the relationship to go and tailor your follow up to meet the goal.

Chapter 13: Online Networking

Though most of this section focuses on in-person networking, it would be careless not to mention online networking which could be just as effective as in-person networking. Assess your immediate network and inventory who your online contacts of colleagues, classmates, and professional association members. This should include people you know personally who may be able to recommend you or point you in the right direction.

Make sure your immediate connections are all inclusive of past and current connections then make an assessment of your secondary contacts. This would include people who you know of but don't know well enough for them to be your immediate contact. Those secondary contacts may be linked to you through your immediate contacts and you should research and categorize those contacts by how relevant they are to your industry and your career goals.

Online Networking Strategy

- Assess your existing immediate network to identify who in your network can help you meet your career goals. In assessing your current network, ask yourself the following questions:
    - How well connected are your contacts?
    - Do they help a lot of people?
    - Are they connectors?
    - How relevant are they to your career goals?

- Create a LinkedIn profile and connect with all of your contacts. If you identify a person who could be very helpful in assisting you with meeting your career goals but it has been awhile since you last spoke to them, reach out via email, LinkedIn, or phone to re-establish the relationship. If they are local, plan to meet in person for an informational interview and be transparent about your goals. Specifically ask them to assist with your career goals and be your advocate along the way.

- Keep in mind the following when reconnecting with a past contact who could be helpful:

    - Get to know them again: Don't approach the relationship with the sole intent of seeking a favor. Establish a genuine connection and be considerate of their time, but be transparent and honest in your intent. Seek to find a balance between asking for assistance and developing the relationship.

    - Ask for guidance or recommendations: This person can serve as a reference or recommend you for open positions they may know of. They can forward relevant jobs to you as they are made available.

    - Remember the rules of business etiquette: You have invited a past contact to meet in order to assist you in your career goals, be sure to respect their time, be prepared, and pay for their meal or coffee. Impressions go a long way and when you are requesting help, a favorable impression can go a long way in getting the results you desire.

    - Ask for introductions: If your immediate contact is not directly connected to your industry but may have people in their network who are, ask for an introduction.

~ Maintain the relationship and be appreciative: Be sure to maintain the relationship even after the career goal is met. It is important not to come off as a person who uses others to get what they want then disappears. Genuine connections and relationships are the goal of networking because your network will always be useful in contributing to your net-worth. Send a thank you note after a meeting. If you met your career goal as a result of their effort, send a gift as a token of appreciation. Send business opportunities their way and remember details about them to assist in the ongoing follow up. Send occasional emails to keep the relationship current and fresh.

DOs & DON'Ts

NETWORKING DOs & DON'Ts

Exchange cards to initiate follow-up & encourage a long-term connections.

Don't aggressively pass out your card to everyone you meet with out developing a genuine connections.

Exchange Cards | Business Cards | Be Aggressive

For in person meetings, eat before you go. Networking is your primary purpose, food is secondary.

Don't over indulge in food or alcohol. Network first and eat small bites as you go.

Eat Before You Go | Eating Etiquette | Over Indulge

Seek to meet new people in your industry who you can provide value to and who may be able to provide future business opportunities.

Refrain from networking only with people you know. Get to know as many new people as possible.

Meet New People | New Contacts | Be Shy

Genuinely connect and develop a strategy to foster a long-term professional relationship. Master the art of "follow-up."

Don't ask for a job or favors when initially meeting someone. Networking is a two-way street.

Follow-up | Conversation | Ask for Favors

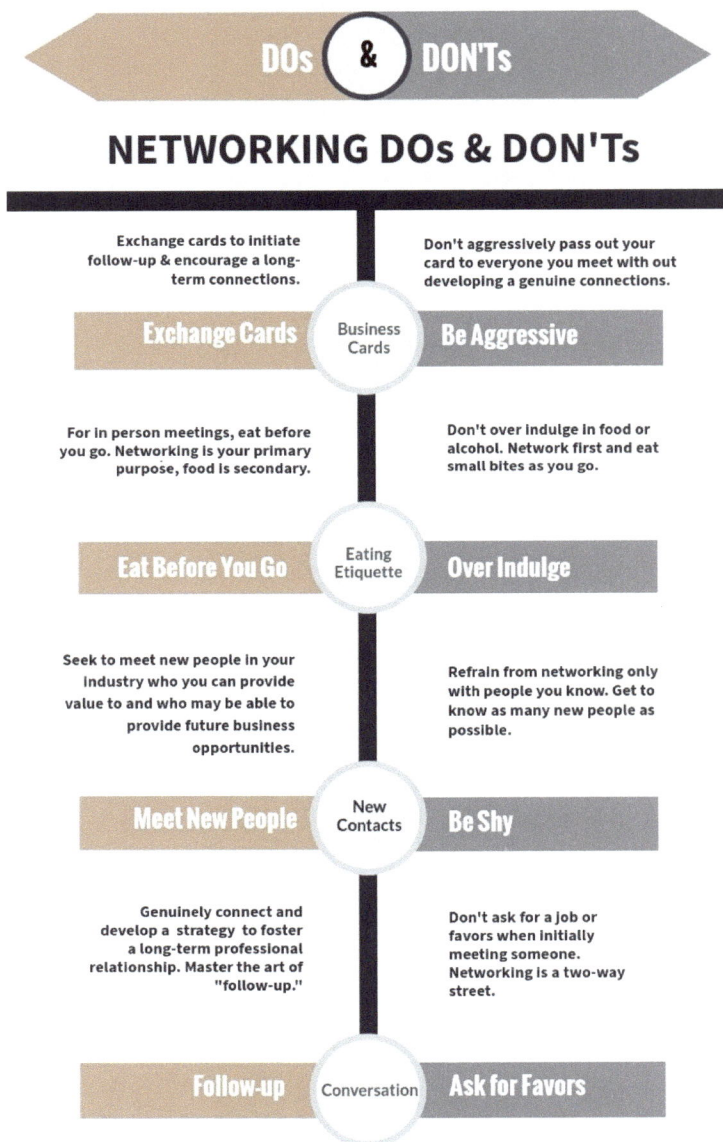

#BrandYourself

CREATED BY
SABRINA MICHELLE COLEMAN

Chapter 14: Networking Action Plan:

NETWORKING ACTION PLAN

1. Professional Goals: Assess your networking goal for each time period.

WEEKLY
NETWORKING
GOALS

MONTHLY
NETWORKING
GOALS

LONG-TERM
GOALS
(9-12 MONTHS)

CURRENT&
FORMER
COLLEAGUES

CURRENT&
FORMER
CLASSMATES

CURRENT/FORMER
CUSTOMERS &
CLIENTS

NETWORKING ACTION PLAN

2. Assess current contacts.

Can your current contacts help you reach your goal? If so, who do you need to reach out to communicate your goals?

Who are the people you would like to connect with? Are there people you know of who you would like to connect with? Are there recent connections who require follow up? Are there people you know who are connected to people you would like to get to know? Assess your network and decide who you need to reach out to.

WHO DO I NEED TO REACH OUT TO?

3. Who did you reach out to?

THIS WEEK	THIS MONTH
Contact:	Contact:
Details:	Details:

NETWORKING ACTION PLAN

4. Who did you recently follow-up with? What is the timeline for the next follow-up?

THIS MONTH

Contact:

Follow-Up Timeline:

5. Have you made recent online connections? If so, document their name and contact information below.

ONLINE CONNECTIONS

Contact:

Details:

6. Have you recently attended professional networking events? If so, document the event, contact info, and specific details of people you connected with.

PROFESSIONAL NETWORKNG EVENTS

Event:

Contact:

Details:

Use this Networking Action Plan regularly to maintain a Rolodex of your connections.

SECTION 5

Differentiation

Chapter 15: Differentiation (Unique Value Proposition)

The previous sections of this book discussed business etiquette, reputation strategy management, authenticity, and networking which all have the commonality of focusing on what you project to the world when managing your brand. This section is literally and figuratively different because it will focus on your unique selling or value proposition and how to stand out in a crowd.

A "unique selling/value proposition" is a marketing term that is used in businesses to help a company distinguish itself from its direct competitors. In many cases, companies will identify a single differentiating factor that they associate with their brand. This factor usually aims to solve a problem, satisfy a need, or relieve a customer's pain point.

When aiming to #BrandYourself professionally, you should work to identify your unique value proposition. This will be the traits or characteristics that separate you from your competition. In a competitive market of homogenous skill sets and degrees, emphasizing your unique value can make the difference between winning or losing business opportunities. The following will assist you in developing an action plan to identify your uniqueness and use it to your competitive advantage.

Unique Value Proposition Action Plan

Step 1: Identify your Uniqueness:

How do you determine your unique value proposition? You have strengths that sets you apart from the competition and will help you stand out from the crowd. It is imperative that you conduct a self-assessment to determine your unique strengths.

IDENTIFY YOUR UNIQUENESS

1. What problem will your skill set or expertise solve for your potential company, client, or customer?

2. What is your level of expertise in that area?

3. Who is your competition?

4. What do you provide that your competition doesn't? What do you do better than your competition?

5. What do you have to offer and how do you offer it?

Once you have identified your uniqueness, you must develop it. Embrace who you are as an individual and develop and polish your identifying characteristics by applying the techniques in the previous chapters. Resist the urge to downplay your individuality and don't try to be who you think other people want you to be. No one else can do things exactly the way you can and you should use this to your advantage. This will contribute to your brand identity.

Step 2: Use your Uniqueness as your Competitive Advantage

Once you have determined your unique strengths, you must strategize on how you can use them to your competitive advantage. There is no one-size-fits-all approach to branding, business, or success, and the final result should be as unique as you are. Your uniqueness should be the foundation of your strategy or brand as it will accentuate your competitive advantage and will make it harder for your competition to emulate what you have to offer.

Uniqueness as a Competitive Advantage

1 CONVENIENCE
2 QUALITY RESULTS
3 EMOTIONAL APPEAL
4 CREATIVITY
5 CUSTOMER EXPERIENCE

#BRANDYOURSELF

Five "Unique" Approaches to developing your Competitive Advantage:

1. **Convenience:** Is it more convenient to work with you over your competition?
1. **Quality Results:** Do you consistently deliver exceptional results? Do you under promise and over deliver?
2. **Emotional Appeal:** Do you appeal to the emotions of your target audience? Will they offer you business opportunities because they want to (indulgent desire) or because they need to (inherent necessity)?
3. **Creativity:** Do you inspire others to think differently and deliver specialized products or services?
4. **Customer Experience:** Do you appeal to potential companies, clients, and customers by offering more than a service, but an experience? Do you connect with customers? Are you in tune with their needs?

There are many examples of public figures who have used their uniqueness to create a competitive advantage that furthers their efforts.

- Former President Barack Obama appealed to the emotions of the American people by selling hope and change during his 2008 election.

- Steve Jobs offered creativity and inspired solutions with his work at Apple.

- Oprah offered a complete customer experience to her audience when she hosted her talk show by consistently showering them with gifts and showing appreciation.

COMPETITIVE ADVANTAGE ASSESSMENT

1. What does your target company, client, or customer want? What need are you satisfying? Put yourself in their shoes to truly assess their needs.

2. What motivates your target audience's business decisions? What are the psychological drivers? Are they motivated by desires or needs?

3. What are the unique features that set you apart that you can promote to make your target market want to do business with you or offer you business opportunities? Think of how you can position your brand to highlight your unique selling/value proposition.

The goal is to make yourself stand out, especially in a market filled with people similar to you. Remember, no one can do what you do the way you do it.

Conclusion

Now that you have read and implemented strategies to #BrandYourself professionally, you should be an expert in all things related to business etiquette, reputation management, authenticity, networking, and differentiation. In case you skipped around or need a quick reference, the following 'Posh Principles' should be used to help you manage your brand.

15 Crucial Posh Principles

1. Stand out for all the right reasons.
2. Focus your position. Don't try to be all things to everyone.
3. In a world riddled with scandal and unscrupulous business practices, being honest and of high integrity can set you apart and give you a competitive advantage.
4. Flattery will get you everywhere. Give compliments, don't upstage, and accept compliments with grace.
5. Respect everyone you meet, from the administrative assistant to the CEO. It can be the crucial factor in obtaining a business opportunity.
6. Be considerate by considering how your actions will affect those around you.
7. Be helpful and be a team player.
8. Be polite. Please, thank you, and you're welcome goes a long way
9. Beware of what your body language says about you. Maintain eye contact, smile, and be approachable.
10. Listen to understand, don't listen to respond and never interrupt. Guard your tongue.

11. Don't complain. Negative people lose opportunities. Complaints are draining and people tend to avoid complainers.
12. Manage expectations: Under promise and over deliver.
13. Be on time and prepared.
14. Follow up and send thank you notes.
15. Speak well of others and don't burn bridges.

About the Author

Sabrina Coleman is an entrepreneur and writer specializing in personal branding. She launched her business etiquette and professional branding strategy business with a mission to help college students, small business entrepreneurs, and young professionals gain a competitive advantage by applying the unwritten rules of success. After being in corporate America for the past 10 years, Sabrina has become acutely aware of the importance of business etiquette and professional branding in career success and she is committed to helping others manage their professional brand.

www.ingramcontent.com/pod-product-compliance
Lightning Source LLC
Chambersburg PA
CBHW041103110426
42740CB00043B/141